Papa Jones

Crystal Jones

DEDICATION

For my husband: William Jones Jr., you are my Superman

For our children: Zachary, Rebekah, Tereaon, Jacob, and Katherine - I love you and am so proud of the people you have become.

For our grandchildren: Cameron, Aubrey, and all that are to come, may what God has started in our lives carry over into your lives for many generations to come.

Acknowledgement:

Special Acknowledgement:

I want to extend a special thank you to Greg and Rosa Boyd. These people have been quiet giants in my life. They decided, years ago, to believe in, and take up the cause of, a single mother just coming into the church.

I can't say the number of times one of them has slipped money into my hands that fed us or put gas into our car. Oftentimes, when I wasn't sure of how either of these things would happen, they would come to my rescue. They have always believed in, and supported, our children in every avenue of ministry they seek to fulfill.

Fast forward several years later, Brother Greg will still hand me cash to send to our college kids just so they can eat a good meal or have a nice weekend. They are dedicated Christians who embody the love of Christ.

Brother Greg is also a leader at the homeless ministry for our church. I have learned so much about love and sacrifice through this ministry. It has afforded everyone in our family a platform to grow in ministry and the Word. I am so thankful for him and the entire Hope team's dedication to the homeless of Atlanta. I couldn't imagine my life without this ministry. It is a huge part of my family.

Thank you!

CONTENTS

FOREWORD

As you read through the pages of this story, I pray that the characters touch your heart, and that the Word of God enlightens your soul. We are made overcomers by the word of our testimony. Never hesitate to share what God has done in your life.

"And they overcame him by the blood of the Lamb, and by the word of their testimony, and they loved not their lives unto death" (Revelations 12:11).

Papa Jones may be fictional, but the fun-loving, spiritual-minded, family-oriented, and wonderful man he represents is my best friend and the one true love of my life. I have taken creative liberties within the work, but it is loosely based on my husband's powerful testimony.

1
A TIMELESS TALE

"Babe, come over here and meet your grandson." Mama Crystal beamed from across the room.

Papa Jones picked up the baby. He couldn't hold back the tears. "Well, son, we are going to have some amazing adventures. And don't you worry about anything. Papa will be right here to help you along the way." Papa smiled down at the baby sleeping in his arms.

"Our first grandson. I can't believe this day is finally here. I believe there will be many more grandchildren coming, but this little guy will always hold a special place. He is the beginning of the legacy we have dedicated our lives too. I pray that he never knows a life outside of the Lord. And that he comes to know Jesus at an early age. Let's pray for God's covering and protection over him." Papa gathered his family around and spoke words of faith over his first grandson.

***

Thank you for the opportunity to speak. I give honor to Bishop, the fellow Pastors, and all the Ministry Leaders in the house today. And to all of you. I don't take lightly the invitation or responsibility afforded to me. We have gathered together this afternoon to honor a great man of God. He was a leader, a visionary, a worshipper, an encourager, and a light to many. To us, he was simply Papa Jones.

I have thought, many days, about how to proceed. What words could be used to adequately describe the life of this great man? How can I give him honor? How can I fit into this allotted timeframe the meaning of his life? Quite simply, I can't. I have prayed that God would grant me wisdom and the grace to proceed. I would like to start with prayer. If we could all stand and go to the Lord in prayer.

Dear Lord, I ask that You comfort my family and friends today. Our hearts are broken. Your Word tells us that in You is a peace that surpasses all understanding; Lord, we need that peace today.

Gathered in Your presence today is a body of believers mourning the loss of a saint. We thank You for the time You gave us with Papa Jones. He was a friend to many. He was a wonderful husband to Mama Crystal. By Your grace, he was a dedicated father and grandfather. Lord, please speak through me to provide comfort to this hurting people. Let Your Holy Ghost speak through me today as I lay out the foundation of a life that was bought with a price. A life You saved, cleansed, transformed, molded, shaped, and blessed for the last eighty-five years.

Lord, we give You honor and praise. Thank You for every person gathered here today. And it's in that lovely name of Jesus, we pray.

Thank you. You all may be seated.

The only way I know how to start is by painting a picture for you. I pray that by sharing a little bit of him with you today, we can all begin the process of healing. He always referred to me as his buddy or son. I can still hear his big voice calling out to me. The fishing pond was his pulpit. This old tattered Bible of *his, that I am using today, was what he used to impart hope and love into his family. As I reflected on my own life this week, I realized that there are very few parts of the man I am today that weren't influenced in some way by him.*

2
JUST A BOY

"Who is ready for some fishing?" Papa Jones shouted from the family room. He was greeted with excited squeals from his grandchildren.

"Ok, Mama, we will be back in a little bit and I'm sure we will be starving from all the fishing we are about to do." Papa Jones winked at his wife as he prepared the equipment and ushered the kids from the house.

"You just bring some fish back and I will handle lunch." Mama Crystal closed the door behind them with a smile and got busy in the kitchen.

"Now, Kamden and Ariel," Papa Jones looked over at his grandkids, "tell me how school is going; who are your friends and what is your favorite part of the day?"

"Papa, I really love school. It is fun. All the kids are my friends. My favorite friend is Alex. She is so nice, and we love to color together. My favorite part of the day is coming in and helping my teacher get the class ready." Ariel was very matter-of-fact in her answer.

Now five years old, she had a soft-toned voice, lovely blonde locks, and her small stature and huge personality made her the most adorable child. She grabbed her pink Minnie Mouse pole and got settled in close to Papa Jones.

"I don't know about school. It's ok, I guess. Easton is my best friend. We like to go to the playground," Kamden chimed in as he found his spot a few feet away from his sister.

Kamden had always been a precocious child. He was a ball of energy and asked straightforward questions. He was only seven, but he was extremely independent and curious.

"Papa, do you think you could get a new goat for me? I could help take care of him when I am here." Kamden looked up at his grandpa with wishful anticipation.

"Now, son, you know we already have two; I don't think your Mama Crystal will be happy if I bring home another goat."

"Oh, Papa, she won't mind. Not if he is mine and I help with him," Kamden stated sure he could convince Mama Crystal it was a great idea.

"Did I ever tell you guys about my pet goat Susie?" Papa Jones started with a smile.

"No. Papa, did Susie live on your farm when you were little?" both kids asked as they settled in for one of Papa's stories.

"Well, I didn't really live on a farm. It was out in the country where I grew up. I lived in a small town called Griffin, Georgia. It was me, my mom, and my dad. I had other animals, but Susie was my favorite. She used to laugh at me!" Papa knew that would get their attention.

***

This is how I remember most weekends my sister and I spent with our grandparents. Papa Jones and Mama Crystal's house was our favorite place to be growing up. They lived on a few acres in North Georgia.

Papa Jones was a semi-retired truck driver; at the time, he was running his business, but no longer in the truck. His pride and joy was a small pond that he kept well stocked with fish. He spent most days out there with a fishing pole and his Bible. The weekends Ariel, my younger sister, and I spent on that little farm were valuable in so many ways.

Papa Jones loved to have talks with us about life. He was always quick with a story and biblical explanation that related to what we were dealing with.

Mama Crystal always had a smile on her face and was a phenomenal cook. She taught lessons from the kitchen as often as Papa taught them from the pond. Their love was one for the record books and was blessed by God.

I learned to love and care for my wife by watching their example. They were the type of people who didn't have to tell you they were Christians. If you were around them for more than five minutes, you knew it.

They always took time to make us feel special. We went on many grand adventures, but they always made time for some form of ministry involvement. There were very few weekends with our grandparents that we weren't taken to the homeless ministry, the nursing home, or a bible study or two; most weekends, we did all of these things together.

Cookouts and "family" dinners were grand events. Everyone looked forward to them. There were always more church family members in attendance than natural family. My grandparents would take time to make everyone feel special and loved. The conversations were mostly about the Lord, and a little football during the season if you joined the men on the back deck. I saw them many times pray with one family or another as they spoke with them privately in the driveway before they left for their own homes. They were never embarrassed or too busy for a prayer with a friend.

I remember when I was younger, and had picked up some songs from friends at school that contained a few questionable lyrics, Mama Crystal was quick to remind me that at their house we only sang about Jesus. A rule she readily enforced with many trips to the corner for me.

They were who they said they were, no matter who was around. It never mattered what day of the week it was, because they were on a mission every day to be true to the Lord they loved.

***

"Papa, goats don't laugh!" Both kids looked at their grandpa like he was crazy.

"That is exactly what Mama Crystal used to say until my dad told her about Susie. She never believed the stories I told until she got his confirmation. For your information, goats do laugh. Susie would crinkle up her lip and laugh at you. One time, I was looking at some new puppies under our porch and Susie came up behind me very quietly. I was leaned over on my hands and knees when Susie headbutted me. She sent me flying face first into the dirt." Papa Jones could barely speak through the laughter as he recanted the tale. "She thought it was hilarious to see me go soaring."

"She also didn't like my mama. She would eat all her flowers, but would never touch my dad's. One time, we had some family come over; that Susie was better than any guard dog and she wouldn't let them out of the car." Papa and the kids were now laughing out loud as he acted out Susie's guard dog techniques.

"I want a goat just like Susie. Did you keep her forever?" Kamden asked jumping up to check his pole.

"No, son, you will find in life that most things aren't forever. Just like we have summer, fall, and winter, there are seasons in life. Like now, you and your sister are in a season, but soon you will grow up and be very different than you are right now. You will get old. Kamden will get smelly. Ariel will get bossy. I am just joking, but you will both change.

"Sadly, my poor Susie had to leave our home because she made my mama mad one too many times." Papa Jones sat down and pulled his Bible from his tackle box. It was always a good time for a lesson.

"Now, kids, the Bible tells us," Papa opened the Word, "To everything, there is a season and a time to every purpose under heaven" (Ecclesiastes 3:1). It also lets us know that we will grow, not only physically, but also spiritually."

Papa checked his and Ariel's poles and continued, "When I was a child, I spake as a child, I understood as a child, I thought as a child: but, when I became a man, I put away childish things" (1 Corinthians 13:11).

"Papa, I don't want to grow up. Grownups are always working and they don't have any fun." Kamden plopped down next to the pond.

"Now, that isn't true. We are having fun today, aren't we?" Papa Jones secured his pole and went to sit beside his young grandson. "It is true that we have to work when we grow up, but that is a blessing. God made man to work. It is what He designed us to do. There are very specific jobs that men and women must do. Being a grownup is just as fun as being a kid; we just have fun in different ways."

Papa Jones picked up the Bible to validate his point. He was always careful to let his grandkids know where his wisdom came from. "And the Lord God took the man and put him into the Garden of Eden to dress it and keep it" (Genesis 2:15).

The trio gathered up their equipment and made their way back to the house. They all caught a whiff of the wonderful smells coming from the kitchen. Those aromas sent a roar through all of their stomachs.

"Who is hungry?" Mama Crystal had met them at the door. "I have some lunch and dessert ready for us. I want to hear all about the fishing trip. Who caught the most?"

The trio filed into the kitchen and started grabbing for the food.

"Now, wait just a minute; I need to see some hand washing and hear some thanksgiving before you dig in." Mama Crystal sent them scurrying for the sink.

"Mama Crystal," Kamden struggled to speak with his mouth full, "how would you feel about me getting a goat? I would take care of him when I am here. I wouldn't let him eat your flowers or laugh at you!"

All four of them burst out laughing.

"I see Papa has been telling stories again." Mama Crystal winked over at her husband. "I think Papa and I will need to discuss it further and we will let you know."

The grandkids and Papa Jones knew that was the end of any discussion for now on that subject.

"You will all be excited to know that Uncle Jake and Aunt Terry will be visiting in the next few weeks," Mama Crystal couldn't hide her excitement, "and we need to plan a big welcome home party for them."

They spent the rest of the afternoon planning the party.

***

Papa Jones and Mama Crystal had four children. The two boys were Mama Crystal's sons. My dad and my Uncle Jake. My dad handles the business for Papa's trucking company. Uncle Jake is a missionary to South America. He always brought home the best gifts and told amazing stories. I remember that I couldn't wait to be old enough to go and visit him.

Papa Jones had two daughters: Aunt Terry, who is a Pastor's wife in another state and Aunt Kathy, who is a year younger than me.

We never really thought much about the dynamics of our family. They were just our family and the circumstances seemed normal to us.

As I got older, I realized the powerful testimony that was behind the shaping of our family. God is so good, and I am glad He was in control of their lives long before I came along.

At least once a year, Uncle Jake and his family were able to come back to the States for a visit. We always made a big deal out of it. These family gatherings were so much fun.

My dad and Papa Jones spent hours on the grill, usually with me trying to help in some way. Mama Crystal, my mom, and Aunt Terry had the kitchen smelling so wonderful. Aunt Kathy and Ariel could usually be found with the ladies learning to cook and enjoying their conversations.

These gatherings usually meant dessert any time of the day you wanted it. The whole farm was full of laughter and full of food!

***

"I'm just a boy!" Kamden's face grew red as he answered Papa's question. "I don't have a girlfriend. Girls are disgusting."

Papa Jones just laughed at the answer. He looked at Mama Crystal and winked.

"Papa, was Mama Crystal your first girlfriend?" Ariel asked from her chair in front of the fireplace.

"No, dollie girl, she wasn't. But, she has been my only girlfriend for more years than I can remember now. And she is the forever girlfriend that God gave me." Papa rose to stoke the fire and sat back down next to a still sulking Kamden.

"When I was young, there was a girl in my neighborhood that would lock me in her barn. She would always tease me that she would never let me out. That girl terrified me." Papa gave a nervous laugh. "I used to tease Mama Crystal about being like that little girl. Once I found her, I was locked up and could never get out."

Mama Crystal shook her head and gave Papa a smile. "Yes, and to God be the glory."

Papa Jones chimed in with a hearty amen and turned his attention back to Kamden. "I know you don't like girls now, son, but one day you will. I was just teasing you about the girlfriend. You know you should never look for just a random girlfriend anyway."

Kamden looked up at his grandpa. "Sure, you should when you're old enough."

Papa smiled and grabbed the Bible from the shelf. "No, young people shouldn't date people just to date them. You must be diligent to stay focused on God and He will direct you in the right way where girls are concerned. I am not saying you can't be friends with girls, but dating is more serious and should be taken seriously.

"When you get really interested in girls, it should be because you are ready to look for a wife. You will ask yourself if that woman fits into the calling God has on you, and whether or not you can see yourself being in ministry with her for the long run. You find her in the prayer room, son, and you will never be sorry."

Mama Crystal sat some warm cookies down on the coffee table. "I know it probably doesn't make sense now, but we live by a different set of rules than the rest of the world."

Kamden chimed in, "Yes, we are different because we are Christians."

"Exactly," both grandparents stated.

Papa Jones began to read, "Neither do men light a candle and put it under a bushel, but on a candlestick; and it giveth light unto all that are in the house" (Matthew 5:15).

Mama Crystal interjected, "It may not make sense now, but there is a reason why we live the way we do in contrast to the world." To that, she added, "And be not conformed to this world: but be ye transformed by the renewing of your mind, that ye may prove what is that good, and acceptable, and perfect, will of God" (Romans 12:2).

"Papa, is that why we dress differently?" Ariel asked through a mouthful of cookies.

Papa picked up his Bible and started reading, "The woman shall not wear that which pertaineth unto a man, neither shall a man put on a woman's garments: for all who do so are an abomination unto the Lord thy God" (Deuteronomy 22:5).

Papa continued, "The Bible gives us instructions on how to be men and women. God speaks very honestly about everyone doing what they are supposed to do. There are certain things that are for the man and others that are for the woman.

"When God made humans, he made them male and female or man and woman. There is nothing in-between. The world will tell you all kinds of things, but you trust in

God and His Word and you will never be confused about what is right and wrong. I know you guys may hear some things at school that don't exactly match what you hear at home and church. It may seem a little puzzling now especially because we look, act, and conduct ourselves differently than the people around us.

"But, what you must remember is that Christians don't belong to this world. We belong to Jesus. The Bible tells parents to train their children in the way they should go. It is our job to make sure you know about the Lord. The Bible also lets us know that God puts spiritual authority in our lives, like Pastors, to help us discern or know clearly how to interpret the Word. With that commandment, the Lord also gives a promise. He says if we train you according to the Bible, when you are old, you won't depart from it. That is why it is so important to read and know the Bible for yourself.

"One day, being Christian won't be something your parents, grandparents, or the church is training you to be, but it will be something that you will be because you know and love the Lord for yourselves." Papa sat down next to Kamden and continued, "I want you guys to study the Scriptures and know them for yourselves. And never stop asking questions if you don't understand something.

"You need to know why we dress as we do. Just saying that you dress differently because it is what your church does or your parents do is not the right answer. For now, while you are young, it may be your answer, but when you get older, you should know for yourselves. We can't be a witness to others if we don't even know why we believe what we believe. How about we start a little Bible study next week to talk about some of the ways we live holy?" Papa closed his Bible.

Kamden looked up from his fourth cookie. "I would like that, Papa. I do have a few questions about some things I heard. And

I may need to know a little more about this dating thing, for future reference, of course; girls are still gross."

Mama Crystal smiled at her grandkids as she picked up the remaining cookies from the table. "Great! I love a good Bible study. I am so excited that you are both starting Bible quizzing. We will do a little Bible study and quizzing practice next weekend. Now, who wants to go for a walk to the pond before dark?"

***

In every season of my life, I can remember a time when a visit to Papa Jones's house made the difference. The laughter and love they shared with us was a priceless treasure.

Now, as a father and a Pastor, I can appreciate so much the biblical values that were instilled in me from an early age. I try, as Papa Jones always did, to make sure that I back up my opinions with biblical principles when making a point to my own children.

I make time for God first and my family second; a principle that Papa Jones always put into practice. Papa Jones, and Uncle Jake, always said that being a minister is about being a servant. The pulpit is not where you do most of your work.

He told me years later, as I began to work out my calling, that God has a specific place for everyone in the body. We are all called to minister, preach, and teach. He was so thankful when God called me.

I know that the hours of prayer that went up to Heaven, for Ariel and me, from Papa Jones and Mama Crystal helped us both along the way. It is my daily desire that others would see Christ in me, as I always saw Him in my Papa Jones.

3
RESPECT

"Did you guys know that your papa was terrified when we had our first kiss?" Mama Crystal exclaimed as she sat down with her coffee.

"Now, honey, we don't have to tell that story." Papa Jones sighed knowing it was already too late. "Ok, I guess we do, since our Mister Kamden is preparing to take this young girl out."

Kamden stood ready to defend himself. "Papa, I remember what I have been taught. I am not dating just to date. This girl is special. I can see her as someone God means for me to marry. She is always praying for the lost and works hard in ministry. And we are just going to talk. There will be no kissing for a long time. I know who and Whose I am. And

I am more than aware of Whose she is too. She is always reminding me." Kamden went on in a huff, "Besides, I see how some of the other guys bounce around from this girl to that one. I hear how the girls talk about them. They are making a bad name for themselves and don't even realize it. They seem to never be satisfied with one girl for very long. I think they don't know who they are or what they want and that hurts them when they try to get into relationships. I am not interested in being that guy."

Ariel chimed in, "And, of course, she is so beautiful, at least that is all Kamden really talks about."

They all laughed, and Papa replied, "I know you have put some thought into this, son, and I am glad you don't take it lightly. I was scared on my first date with Mama Crystal. I knew she was a woman of God.

"I was just getting back into church at the time. We had been having long talks on the phone for a few weeks and I knew she was special. We had gone for a walk down at the park. We walked and talked, and it was a nice time. We stopped by the river, and out of nowhere, we kissed. As soon as I did it, I was terrified. I thought that lightning would strike me.

"Here I was new to the church, a backslider just coming home, and I was out with this prayer warrior, kissing her of all things. It was a small kiss, but I was seriously waiting to be struck down as we walked back to the car."

Mama Crystal chuckled as she replied, "Now, we were much older than the two of you. But, he looked terrified as we walked back to the car. When he finally told me what was wrong, I couldn't help but laugh. I was very glad he thought that highly of me.

"A woman should always conduct herself in a manner that suggests she is a holy vessel of the Lord. I didn't admit it, but I was scared also. I hadn't imagined ever having feelings toward any man after coming back to church. I had a rough time being lost out in the world and was content to just serve the Lord for the rest of my life and forget about relationships.

"But, God. He had a different plan for me. One that was far better than any I could have imagined. You will find, my loves, that His plans are always better than our own. We just have to have the faith to wait on Him."

Papa pulled out the Bible and asked Kamden to read, "Rebuke not an elder, but entreat him as a father; and the younger men as brethren; the elder women as mothers; the younger as sister, with all purity" (1 Timothy 5:1-2).

He then had Ariel read, "In like manner also, that women adorn themselves in modest apparel, with shamefacedness and sobriety…" (1 Timothy 2:9).

She passed the Bible over to Aunt Kathy. "So ought men to love their wives as their own bodies. He that loveth his wife loveth himself" (Ephesians 5:28).

Papa Jones followed up, "Now, I know it is just grabbing some coffee, or whatever, and I know you are a good young man. But, let's pray that you will be able to follow the Lord's will for your life, no matter what your flesh wants you to do. Let's also pray that you, and this young woman, are hedged up and protected by God. We want your witness and walk to be pure."

***

As we prayed that night, I felt God move into the family room. I couldn't have known it then, but those prayers were protecting my future wife and me from hardships that we were never going to have to face, as we dated and eventually married.

God, as He always does, already had a plan for me. I am so thankful for the effectual prayers of my grandparents that, no doubt, kept me from the many mistakes I should have made.

I wasn't perfect then and, certainly, am not now. In fact, I am far from it, but I am forever growing in grace. If you have godly examples in your life, please don't take them for granted.

One of my favorite memories of my grandparents has always been watching and listening to them read the Word together. They had started reading the Bible together daily before they were married and continued for the remainder of their time together.

Papa Jones and Mama Crystal were to me, what I strive to be for my family and all of you: a constant source of strength and stability hedged about with prayer and having an earnest walk with the Lord.

***

"Wonderful, I can feel the presence of God." Papa Jones stood and moved to a seat closer to his grandchildren. "Do you know that I found God when I was not much older than you?" Papa grabbed his coffee as he made the statement.

"Dad, I thought you grew up in church? Can you tell us about finding God? "Aunt Kathy plopped down next to Ariel with great interest.

For the first time in their young lives, he shared his testimony with his grandchildren and his youngest daughter. "My mama passed away when I was just a teenager. It was a very difficult thing for my dad and me to deal with. She had been sick for a long time. As a young man, I had to spend many evenings helping to care for her. Caring for a sick relative, especially a mother, can be a difficult chore for a teenager. I was with her in the hospital room when she passed away.

"Shortly after she died, I went to live with my aunt. I went from a very country life to a city life. The transition was a difficult one for me. I was a beast on the football field, but no match for the city streets. I was heartbroken and scared without my mom, but I was trying to act so tough.

"It wasn't long before I got into drugs. I started selling drugs, as well as doing them. I stayed in trouble with the law. After going to jail a few times, I got into some major trouble and was looking at doing some hard time in prison. It was during this time that I found the Lord.

"I tried many other types of religion while in jail. I was introduced to several philosophies, but none had the power to change me. Then, I got into trouble inside the jail. I made a deal with God. I told Him that if He would spare me from the punishment I was sure to receive, I would truly seek after Him. To my amazement, that was exactly what He did. From that time on, I began to seek after the Lord with joy. I read the Bible several times and attended the services that they provided for the inmates.

"One afternoon on the prison yard, a few of the men encouraged me to seek after the Holy Ghost; I lifted my arms to Heaven and was filled that afternoon. I began to speak in a language I never knew. I had read in the Bible that this was the evidence of the infilling of the Holy Ghost." Papa's voice quivered slightly at the recanting of his testimony. "For with stammering lips and another tongue will he speak to his people" (Isaiah 28:11).

"Dad, what an amazing testimony you have. I never knew. God is so awesome. He knew you weren't a bad guy. I am so glad He changed you so we could all be here right now." Aunt Kathy moved over to give her dad a hug.

"That's just it, sweetheart; I was a bad guy. But God has the power to change us into someone we could never see ourselves being. I was a gang member. I was a person who would beat people up and pull guns on people. There were many times I could have, and should have, killed someone. I was busy trying to make and maintain my reputation in the streets. That life comes with a price." Papa Jones returned her hug. "It is only the redemptive power of Christ that had the power to transform me from a thug to a decent man. I know you always hear me quote 1 Corinthians 15:10. I say it because it is so true." Papa smiled and quoted the Scripture, "But by the grace of God I am what I am."

"Papa, did you walk with the Lord from that time on?" Kamden asked with genuine curiosity.

"Sadly, no, son. I have failed God many times over the years. But, He has never left me. When I got myself together and started doing what I knew to do, He was always right there." Papa Jones grabbed his Bible from the coffee table.

"Be strong and of good courage, fear not, nor be afraid of them: for the Lord thy

God, he it is that doth go with thee; he will not fail thee, nor forsake thee" (Deuteronomy 31:8).

Papa continued, "The Word clearly lets us know that God will never leave us. Many people walk away from God, but He will never walk away from us." Papa smiled over at his wife and continued, "For I am persuaded, that neither death, nor life, nor angels, nor principalities, nor powers, nor things present, nor things to come, nor height, nor depth, nor any other creature, shall be able to separate us from the love of God, which is in Christ Jesus our Lord" (Romans 8:38-39).

"Thankfully, the Lord had provided a space of grace for me to be able to make it back to Him. Still, one of my greatest regrets in life is that my decisions caused me to be estranged from my children. God's design for the family is so perfect. I am so thankful I was granted the opportunity to be a father, but one can't help but to wonder how it would have been if I had lived in His will. We pray that when all of you get ready for families, you will do it God's way. He can bless what we have broken, but how wonderful it is to do it the right way from the start." Papa closed his Bible.

Kamden chimed in, "Yes, Papa, that is what my dad always says. The Lord was right there waiting when he decided to come home. He always says he is so thankful that he didn't wait too long to get right."

Mama Crystal stood to refill coffee and hot chocolate cups. "Yes, honey, many people spent many years praying for your dad. It is very important that we don't give up on praying for people who aren't in a right relationship with God. If we are persistent in prayer and faithful, the Lord will continue to draw them to Him. You know I got in church after being out for many years because as a young teenage boy, your daddy prayed for me."

Papa looked down at his watch. "Kamden, I know you have to go, but remember, just as I was lost and then found, a greater testimony lies in those who never stray. God can trust and use you because your life is a testament to faithfulness. It is our desire that all three of you never walk out from under the umbrella of God's covering. He can use you and the testimony of faithfulness to speak to many."

They all concluded with an amen as Kamden left for his date, and the girls retired to the other room to finish their snacks and get their hair ready for Sunday.

***

"They make me so angry," Kamden shouted as he threw the feed bucket across the yard.

Papa walked over from where he was feeding Susie. "Now, wait a minute, son. There is no reason to act that way. What has got you so hot?"

Kamden apologized and went to pick up the bucket. "It's Joy's parents. They are just ridiculous. They act like I'm some crazy person after their daughter. They don't take into consideration how we feel. We are not children. We love the Lord. We pray together and neither of us wants to ruin the other's reputation. Why can't they just let us be?"

Papa smiled and shook his head. "Now, son, sometimes you have to put yourself in the other person's shoes. Let's assume Joy was Ariel. How would you feel about a young man coming around spending so much time with her?

"They are having the same reaction I'm sure I will have when a young man comes around looking for Kathy, or your dad will when Ariel gets a call. I remember when Uncle John started being interested in Aunt Terry." Papa chuckled and shook his head. "It's a hard thing for a man to let his little girl go. It doesn't matter how old she is. Her parents are her God-given guardians until she is married. They are doing their jobs."

Papa smiled at his grandson. "If they saw the way you just acted, they certainly would feel that they are justified in their concerns. Have you tried having a conversation with them?"

Kamden looked disgusted at the thought. "What on Earth would we talk about? No, I haven't sat down and talked to them. I mean, I do speak when I pick up and drop off Joy. I went to outreach with them last Saturday, but we were all just working."

Papa continued, "Kamden, how can you expect them to know what a wonderful young man you are if you don't talk to them? You should see if Joy can arrange dinner for you all. Sit down and tell them your plans and where you see yourself in the kingdom. Let them know where Joy fits into those plans. Tell them what you think of their daughter. Invite them for dinner over here. We would love to meet them, or to dinner with your parents."

Kamden moved over to wrestle with his goat Susie. "Papa, I'm not sure I want to do all that. But, I do see how those things might make them take me more seriously. I'm not some random guy trying to mess with their daughter. I really do care about her."

Papa walked over to Kamden. "It is very important that you learn not to let anger or frustration get the best of you. We must walk in temperance as Christians. It took me many years to be able to control my anger. It is one of the hardest battles a man fights. It is especially hard when you feel that someone you love, or something you love, is under attack. Remember, we do all as unto the Lord. He says to cast your cares on Him. That means take your feelings and concerns to Him in prayer. He is your friend and you can talk to Him as such. Ask Him for wisdom and He will provide it."

The pair put Susie back in the gate with the other goats and made their way towards the house. They could both smell something wonderful coming from the kitchen.

"I want to share something with you that I haven't told very many people." Papa turned to his grandson with a very serious expression. "I used to have anger issues. The Lord really had to work on me in this area. I also had to deal with some pride, as most men do. But, the Lord had to teach me humility. It was a lesson hard learned. When I was in my twenties, I got the opportunity to become a licensed minister. I was honored, but I didn't take the position as seriously as I could have.

"I grew complacent and even felt entitled. I forgot to make God my priority and instead found myself making my position my priority. It led to a very great downfall. Many young men who looked up to me were hurt when I fell. My loving and knowing the Lord didn't excuse my not putting His commandments first in my life. Prayer, fasting, love, and yes, humility must be on the forefront of your mind daily."

Papa and Kamden sat on the back porch. "When I fell away from church, it was a dark time in my life. However, when I came back and started walking with Him again, I vowed to get it right. It wasn't long after that I met your grandmother. Mama Crystal was great, and we had an instant connection. But I was very new to the church." Papa leaned closer to his grandson.

"After only three months of dating, we decided to get married. Both of us were in our late thirties, but it was a concern to our Pastor and the leaders of the church. They didn't know me. They did, however, know her and some of her history. They voiced their concerns to us. Now, both of us knew that we were in love. We knew that it was different and we were putting God first.

"We tried to talk to them and tell them how we felt, but they asked us to wait. Unfortunately, we didn't listen. We went on, without their blessing, and got married." Papa pressed forward, hoping this would help. "Now, thank God, our marriage has been wonderful and blessed. But, that moment of disappointment from our leaders is not something that was easily overcome.

"We had to work very hard after that to gain their trust back. I know that as blessed as we have been, we could have been even more blessed had we listened to the counsel and instruction of our leaders in Christ. Their blessings on our marriage would have made it more joyous." Papa went on, "Years later, in my forties, I heard our old Pastor preach one of the best sermons I ever heard. It was during The Mentorship Conference that we love to attend every year.

"He said if you were to sum the whole Bible up into one word, it would be submission. Everything begins and ends with submission. That was a revelation that I hadn't received in all my years of ministry. Suddenly, every failure in my life could be summed up within those parameters. When I had failed, it was because I wasn't submissive. As a minister, I was still responsible for being submissive to my Pastor and those to whom I preached. And, of course, first and foremost, to God.

"You know who you are, but does your level of submission equal what you know to be true in your heart? Are you walking what you profess to live? I am asking these questions so you will begin to examine yourself and your actions in light of what you feel.

"What I'm trying to say is that if you will take the time to get to know her parents and put their worries and fears at ease, your relationship will be blessed. You won't have the stress of wondering what they are thinking. You won't have the concern of what they are going to be saying to Joy when you're not around. Her parents are her spiritual leaders and you should respect that. One day, you may have a daughter and you will, no doubt, want the same respect from her suitor." Papa finished with tears in his eyes.

Kamden shook his head. "When you're right, you're right. Thanks so much for sharing that with me, Papa. I had no idea you and Mama Crystal were such rebels back in the day. Seriously though, I can see how doing anything to make Pastor, or any of the leadership, distrust you would be an awful place to be in. I don't want to put Joy, or myself, in that position. I will try to speak with her parents and be more cautious about their feelings.

"Perhaps, we should also talk with the Youth Pastor and just let him know about our relationship. Maybe he can give us some insights on how to conduct ourselves in a godly manner for all people involved. I certainly don't want either of our walks to be tainted by my bad attitude."

Mama Crystal opened the back door and started to yell out that dinner was finished. She was startled by the fact that they were already on the back porch. "Well, you two must have smelled it cooking." She chuckled. "I don't know what is so serious out here, but there are some hot biscuits with your names on them."

With that, they all retired to the kitchen.

***

I never thought about life or relationships the same after that talk with Papa Jones. I hadn't taken the time to consider anybody's feelings but my own.

Of course, we all get like that at times. Thankfully, Joy's parents and I have a wonderful relationship. We are honest and open with each other. I am hopeful that when my baby girl gets old enough for a potential husband to come calling, many-many moons from now, I will be patient with the young man.

I had seen Papa Jones and Mama Crystal walk with integrity so many years that I was shocked by his account of the start of their marriage. I know they love, support, and honor Pastor and the church leadership. I can only hope that if I were ever put in a similar situation, God would grant me the grace to redeem myself, as He did for them.

The Word says, "And I give you pastors according to mine heart, which shall feed you with knowledge and understanding" (Jeremiah 3:15).

Pastors and church leaders are our covering. They have been ordained by God to provide us with knowledge and understanding. We should reverence and honor them as our spiritual leaders and advisors.

The times when we feel that we have it all figured out or know everything there is to know are the times we need to be seriously seeking the face of God. We can't know what is best for our own lives.

Sometimes it is especially hard for those of us who grow up in the church. This is the only lifestyle we have ever known. We have heard preaching and teaching from the Bible since before we had the ability to understand it. We have to fight to make it precious and personal to us. At least I did.

Sometimes my questions and concerns, and yes, even my bad attitudes were a surprise to my family. I think because they just assumed I knew the right thing to do. But, knowing God intellectually is a whole lot different than knowing Him personally. Our relationship with Him takes work. It is a daily walk. It has to be done on purpose.

We should judge according to His standards. Only God has the perfect plan laid out for our lives.

"For I know the thoughts that I think toward you, saith the Lord, thoughts of peace, and not of evil, to give you an expected end"(Jeremiah 29:11).

4
CALLING AND ELECTION SURE

"Wherefore the rather, brethren, give diligence to make your calling and election sure: if ye do these things, ye shall never fail" (2 Peter 1:10). Kamden read on, "I press toward the mark for the prize of the high calling of God in Christ Jesus" (Philippians 3:14).

Mama Crystal gave his arm a squeeze. "Thanks so much. Are you sure about dinner?"

Kamden was already headed for the door. "Yes, ma'am. You just rest and feel better. We got this."

With Mama Crystal sick, it was on Kathy, Ariel, and Kamden to make dinner that evening. They made some delicious hamburgers and fries and joined Papa at the lake for some evening fishing.

"Dad, do you think Mama Crystal is ok?" Kathy asked with genuine concern.

"Sure, baby, we'll go back to the doctor on Tuesday and should get a better idea of what is going on. But, I am sure she is fine." Papa made the statement, but his eyes told a different story. His wife had been sick more often lately. He wasn't sure what was going on, but he trusted God.

"Ariel, I know your chorale tour starts in a couple of weeks. We are going to send you some money so you have a great time. And Kathy, I'm sure you are all set for school. Mama Crystal did remind me that we have to pick up a few more things before you leave."

Both girls replied with "thank you."

"Kamden, that just leaves you, son. With Kathy and Ariel headed off to Bible college, it's going to be lonely around here. I'm glad you will be sticking around."

Kamden jumped up and grabbed his pole. "Got a bite! Yes, sir, I am starting next week at Joy's dad's company. He says I will be on the floor for a few weeks and then he will teach me the office stuff. Sounds like a pretty good opportunity. Joy is busy with wedding plans. I will miss these girls while they are gone, but not as much as Joy will."

Papa Jones cut the fish off Kamden's line and checked Kathy's pole. "I still can't believe you are almost a married man. It just blows my mind. I can still see you as a little scrap of a boy chasing me around.

"You know Uncle Jake has invited us to visit him in Bolivia at the end of the month. Mama Crystal isn't willing to go because she wants to be here to get the girls off to school. So, we were thinking it would be a nice opportunity, if you're interested, for you to make the trip."

Kamden jumped up and down. "Are you serious?! Oh my, Papa Jones, I don't know what to say. I am so excited."

Papa Jones smiled at the young man in front of him. Where had the time gone? "Now, of course, you will need to check with Joy's dad since you will be new to the job. And clear it with your parents and Joy. But, yes, I would love for you to make the trip with me."

***

"I'm so excited. It will be eight hours before we land, Papa." Kamden took his window seat on the plane.

"Yes, I'm going to get some reading in and then catch a nap." Papa Jones opened his Bible.

"Papa, how do you know if you are called? Or what you're called to do? I mean, as Christians, we are called to minister to people. We all serve in some capacity. How does a pastor, evangelist, or missionary distinguish their call from that?" Kamden turned to his grandfather in anticipation.

"I can see you have been wrestling with this question. Let's first go to the Word: 'And he gave some, apostles; prophets; and some, evangelist; and some, pastors and teachers; for the perfecting of the saints, for the work of the ministry, for the edifying of the body of Christ'" (Ephesians 4:11-12).

Papa Jones flipped through the Bible in his lap. "In Acts chapter 6, we see that the disciples picked men who were honest, and full of the Holy Ghost to minister to the people. Every person gets their calling at different times in different ways. Also, 1 Timothy Chapter 3 gives specific instructions for specific offices or callings.

"For me, it happened when I was about your age. I felt in prayer a strong urge that God had a different avenue for me. He gave me sermons and words. I started as a servant and God allowed men to promote me."

Kamden chimed in, "Yes, sir. I have heard Uncle Jake, many times, say that even though he felt a call early in his teen years, he always tried to be a servant. He looked for opportunities to serve and not just pulpit time.

"My dad has also told me about his calling. God gifted him with a voice to sing, musical ability, and a way with words. He felt a call in his teens. He said that even though he ran from the call for many years, it was always with him. He saw Uncle Jake walking out his calling and wondered if he had been a better, or stronger man, where his life would have taken him. He said he can't have any regrets because the path he chose led him to Mom, and us. But, he does regret that he didn't fulfill his call from an early age. He says what you always say, that God can take what we break and make it whole."

Papa Jones smiled at this. "Yes, son. And amen. Are you asking for a specific reason?"

Kamden looked at the floor. A little unsure of himself, he said, "I feel something. I don't know yet what it is. But, when I pray, I feel a powerful tug. It is like God is wanting more from me. Sometimes I read the Word and I feel a message or something rising from what I'm reading. But, then, I feel like I am just making it up. That may be because you, Dad, and Uncle Jake are called; I feel like I should be too. I'm just not sure what it all means. Is that crazy, Papa?"

Papa Jones took his grandson's hand. "No, it's not crazy. In fact, I think it is wonderful. Never doubt yourself, or what God is trying to do through you. If God is calling you to a specific ministry or role, He will confirm it in His time. He will also equip you for the work. That is sometimes the hard part. It requires waiting, and sometimes testing and pruning, which can be pretty uncomfortable.

"In the meantime, you should continue to do what you know to do. Don't back down. And ask Him. When you pray, ask Him for direction. I think it is no accident that you are going on this trip. I believe God has a true visitation waiting in Bolivia for you."

The pair prayed quietly and prepared for takeoff.

***

That trip did truly change my life. I saw ministry in a way I had never seen it before. What my Uncle Jake and all the other foreign missionaries do around this world is miraculous.

I saw God do things in that country I had never seen in a lifetime at church in the US. I pray that we can change that.

The worship and unfaltering trust those people had in the astounding power of God was amazing. They walked miles to get to a make-shift building believing that God would meet them there. And He did.

The job of a missionary, much like a pastor, is 24/7. It never stops. The people are always in need. They must pray always for direction and protection. There is always a next task to complete.

Papa Jones and I worked hard while we were there, but we also saw God perform miracles and change lives. We joined with people who didn't speak our language to pray to God who speaks all languages.

It was in one of these prayer meetings that God confirmed His calling on my life. I heard Him almost audibly say that I would preach His gospel and give my life to service for Him.

To this, I responded with a resounding "yes, Lord, I will go where You send me." Uncle Jake also gave me the first opportunity I ever had to speak behind a pulpit. He had me lead prayer for several services, and on the last night, I did a short sermonette, which he translated to Spanish.

I have never been more nervous in my life. Papa Jones and Uncle Jake laughed and said they had both felt the same way when they first started.

Upon returning to the states, I talked with my Pastor and began preparation to sit for my license. Joy and I married with ministry in mind. It has been our life's pleasure to serve every day.

***

"Are you nervous?" Papa Jones sat down next to his grandson. Almost the whole family had come into town to see Kamden receive his ordination.

"No, sir. Well, maybe a little. I feel prepared, though. I know God is in control. Uncle Jake called me early this morning and we prayed. I am so glad everyone made it. I know Mama Crystal is happy to have everyone home for a few days." Kamden slid over a chair to allow his wife to sit down.

"Yes, she wouldn't have missed this for the world. It was difficult to get her here, but having Aunt Terry and the rest of the family around is just what she needs." Papa Jones looked over at his wife holding their newest grandbaby. Oh, how he loved that woman.

"How is the treatment going?" Kamden also shot a worried glance over to his grandmother. She looked weak, but happy.

"Let's not worry about that today. It's your day. God is getting ready to do some great things in your life." Papa Jones fished his Bible from under the seat.

"I'm not sure that much will change. I am still working full time at the factory. And now, with a baby on the way, I'm not sure how much more free time I will have to devote. But, I do believe God will make a way. And I'm open to letting Him use us as He pleases." Kamden started feeling the nerves as the Deacons ascended onto the stage to start the ceremony.

***

Laughter erupted from the kitchen. The house was full of family. Everyone was happy.

"I am so glad you are all here. My heart is so full. God is so good. I am so thankful that He has blessed me with such a wonderful, talented, and beautiful family." Mama Crystal stood to address the people who made up her world.

"Now, love, don't get all sentimental right before we eat. This food is smelling too good," Papa Jones teased his wife. "Shall we have the newest member of the ministry lead us in prayer over the food?" Papa turned the floor over to his grandson.

After dinner, the family settled into the living room with dessert and coffee. Papa Jones grabbed his wife's hand. They stood together to make an announcement to the family. "You know we love you guys. We are glad you are all here. And, Jake, thank you for calling in. This weekend has blessed our souls. We are so proud of each of you. What you do for the kingdom and each other every day is a wonderful gift from God.

"Mama Crystal has asked that we use some of this time, while we are all gathered, to let you know what is happening with her. Darling, I will turn it over to you." Papa Jones stood beside his wife.

"Thank you, and I want to amen what has been said. When God pulled me out of darkness and back into His marvelous light, I could have never envisioned this is what He had in mind for me. You are each a gift from Him. Never doubt that."

Mama Crystal let out a long sigh. "As you know, I have been undergoing treatments for cancer, but we found the other day that I am terminal. The treatments aren't working. Yes, we can, and will, continue to pray. Yes, God can perform a miracle. But, if He has chosen for this to be my time, I just want you to know how much I love you. I am so proud of each of you. You have overcome adversity and gotten over yourselves to be what He has called you to be."

Mama Crystal flipped open her Bible. "But I say unto you, love your enemies, bless them that curse you, do good to them that hate you, and pray for them which despitefully use you, and persecute you; that ye may be the children of your Father which is in Heaven: for he maketh his sun to rise on the evil and on the good, and sendeth rain on the just and on the unjust" (Matthew 5:45). We can't understand why God does all of the things He does. Our job is to have faith and trust Him. I belong to the Lord. He saved my life years ago. And I have tried to live in a way that is an offering unto Him since then."

She proceeded through their tears, "We have fought a good fight. But, my body is tired. The treatments have certainly taken a toll. I don't know why God takes some through sickness, and some instantly, and some live out long years and die in peace. It is not for us to know.

"I pray that none of you will be angry or question the Lord about this. Remember He is in control. Every wonderful moment I have been given by Him has been a blessing. Until I take my last breath, I want to praise Him for His wondrous works." Mama Crystal sat down to finish her statement. The girls gathered around her as she quoted, "But now they desire a better country, that is, a heavenly: wherefore God is not ashamed to be called their God: for he hath prepared for them a city" (Hebrews 11:16).

***

We lost our beloved Mama Crystal not long after that. There is, even now, an empty place in our hearts for her. Papa Jones was riddled with grief, but he never faltered in his love and desire for the Lord.

He was strong for all of us. After much prayer and consideration, my wife and I decided to move onto the farm with Papa. This God-ordained move changed the course of our lives forever. We leaned on each other to heal. We relied on each other for fellowship. Then God showed us His plan for this season of our lives.

The Pastor of Papa Jones's small church approached me with an opportunity. He had been desiring to retire for some time. His health was declining, but he said he couldn't leave until he knew who God would send to take over.

After we prayed and fasted, he presented it to the board, and I became the newly appointed Pastor of the assembly where I had grown up. Papa Jones was so happy. He sat in his normal spot on the first row, minus his beautiful wife, but beaming with godly pride, as I delivered my first message to the congregation. We began to settle into life on the farm, and our new role.

Papa Jones remained a constant voice of reason in my life. His wisdom, as it had since I was a small child, never ceased to guide me in the appropriate direction.

His quotes are infamous: "More room outside than in"; well, we won't talk about that one. "Good goobley-goo" was synonymous with a surprise reaction. "I am what I am by the grace of God"; whenever he received a compliment. "It was a reasonable service"; whenever Mama Crystal thanked him for his help.

But, most of all, I love that he always quoted the Bible to us. He never missed an opportunity to input Scripture.

He carried a Bible, and an ACTS 2:38 tract, everywhere he went. "You never know what God has in mind"; when teaching us to be prepared.

On the side of every truck for his company, Apostolic Trucking, was a giant model of that ACTS

2:38 tract. He kept an Apostolic Bible in the truck for all his drivers. He told many stories of the years he spent on the road when people would randomly come up to him to discuss the name of his company or the message on the truck.

I would often mark in my Bible the Scriptures I had heard him quote over the weekend. I spent many hours as a young man studying out those Scriptures and committing them to memory.

The Bible should be part of our vocabulary as Christians. We tend to undermine its influence and power in our lives. But, it is the power and heartbeat of the God we serve. I pray that I portray that in my own life, as I saw Papa Jones do in his.

He was a giver. He gave time, talent, and treasure. He never passed a law enforcement officer, or military person, without saying, "Thank you for your service." I saw him buy meals for many of them.

He and Mama Crystal gave to the church and to people they met. They didn't announce their giving or make a big deal of it. They just did it because that is what we are supposed to do. They sent many kids on mission trips and helped families with bills and car repairs. They would often visit people in the hospital. They called and sent texts to people who had backslidden.

They were friends in the truest sense of the word. Their home was always open to visitors. There was a hot meal, a yummy dessert, and a fishing pole waiting for anyone who happened to stop by.

He taught us early to be diligent with tithes and offerings. "Bring ye all the tithes into the storehouse, that there may be meat in mine house, and prove me now herewith, saith the Lord of hosts, if I will not open you the windows of Heaven, and pour you out a blessing, that there shall not be room enough to receive it" (Malachi 3:10).

He reminded us that everything we have comes from the Lord. We heard him give thanks to God often for the farm, for his family, and all the blessings in his life. We didn't break bread without giving thanks.

We are called to give. He said he doesn't worry about his needs being provided for because God takes care of his family, as He always has. He taught me the value of hard work. He believed that a man ought *to work and provide for his family. "For even when we were with you, this we commanded you, that if any would not work, neither should he eat" (2 Thessalonians 3:10).*

He was a worshipper. In his younger years, so it was in his later years; he loved to worship the Lord. He never went into the shower without singing praises to the top of his lungs. There were many Sunday mornings that we were awakened by his song way before the alarm clock was to sound. If you asked him, he would say he had to worship God. It is what we were made to do. "Give unto the Lord the glory due his name; worship the Lord in the beauty of holiness" (Psalms 29:2).

He could be heard all over the congregation giving praise to God. His laughter was infectious. He never picked up an instrument, but loved to hear my dad and Uncle Jake play their guitars. He would light up whenever Aunt Terry would lift her beautiful voice in worship. When we were young, he would make up silly songs to sing with Aunt Kathy, Ariel, and I.

He always encouraged us to play and sing unto the Lord. Worship was his heartbeat.

"O come, let us worship and bow down: let us kneel before the Lord our maker" (Psalms 95:6).

"Know ye that the Lord he is God: it is he that hath made us, and not we ourselves; we are his people and the sheep of his pasture. Enter into his gates with thanksgiving, and into his courts with praise: be thankful unto him and bless his name. For the Lord is good; his mercy is everlasting; and his truth endureth to all generations" (Psalms 100:3-5).

5
THE FIERY TRIAL

"Papa, I just don't understand what the big deal is. That woman knows I love her. I am a Pastor for Heaven's sake. I am devoted to God and my family. I feel like she is just blowing things out of proportion." Kamden grabbed his fishing pole and began to cast.

"Son, have you talked with her about these things?" Papa sat down on his bucket and fiddled with his lure.

"Of course, I have, Papa. She says she understands that nothing happened but can't understand why I don't think it is a bigger deal. She is so concerned with proving her point that she can't accept mine." Kamden settled on a spot for a final cast and plopped down next to his grandfather in frustration.

"Son, it seems to me that what you are accusing her of is exactly what you are doing. Perhaps, you could ask her to explain it in a different way. Maybe she can help you understand her point of view, but you must be willing to really listen. This may surprise you, but your Mama Crystal and I had some problems at the beginning of our marriage. Our issues were much worse than this situation, however."

Papa reached into the tackle box for his Bible. He was going to need the Lord's help with this one.

Kamden was very interested in hearing this story. "Papa please share with me. I can't imagine you and Mama Crystal ever arguing over anything like this."

Papa Jones cleared his throat and pulled his jacket on. "I knew your Mama Crystal was for me from day one, but I was newly back in church. I also had a situation with your Aunt Kathy. Her mom and I were never married, but I had tried to do the right thing when I found out there was a baby on the way. I had hoped that I could make it work for Kathy's sake. I wanted the opportunity to be there for my child." He continued nervously, "When the relationship with your Mama Crystal started getting serious, I struggled with letting go of my past. I was looking for love in all the wrong places. I had convinced myself that I needed a wife to be happy.

"Of course, what I needed was the Lord. He is peace and joy. All that we need or want is found in Him. And when we are in a relationship with Him, He is so gracious to give us the desires of our hearts. I believed that I knew what it took to be a good husband. I felt that providing for my family and being there for them was enough.

"Your Mama Crystal didn't play games. She expected me to be a true man of God all the way around. As you know, she had been hurt by many men in her past. She was determined to have a relationship steeped in Christian principles and power.

"One of the first times she rode in the truck with me, another girl messaged me on Facebook. I felt that it was harmless to carry on conversations with women I was talking to before she and I were in a committed relationship. I had no intention of doing anything other than speaking with them. Mama Crystal insisted that by carrying on outside conversations, I was ruining my witness with these souls and making her look like a fool. Of course, she was right. Men and women must guard themselves against unseemly situations.

"We have rules of engagement for a reason. Words, text messages, and social media conversations can often be misconstrued into something they were never intended to be." He could see Kamden's eyes getting wider with understanding. "You see, son, whether you mean them to or not, your actions can cause pain to the person you love the most.

"There was one young lady that I had been interested in before I had started dating Mama Crystal. This young lady and I would exchange messages from time to time on Facebook and via text. After I got married, we continued to message each other. It seemed harmless enough to me.

"I never knew that Mama Crystal had seen all the messages that we had exchanged. Some of them were not appropriate. She was also heartbroken every time I liked or commented on that young lady's Facebook posts.

"It took her a while to speak on it, and when she did, I just brushed it off. I didn't want to stop talking to the girl, even though I had no business doing it. The Word tells us, 'But I say unto you, that whosoever looketh on a woman to lust after her hath committed adultery with her already in his heart.'" (Matthew 5:28).

Kamden shook his head. "Mama Crystal was patient and worked with you, even though she was obviously hurt. I see that I must refer to my training and what I know to be right. I can't grow complacent or comfortable. I understand that I have let myself get familiar and have been too trusting."

Papa Jones sighed. "Son, I believe you are alright to trust, but you have to always remember your place. You are God's first and Joy's second. You may have the best of intentions, but you must always be aware of how things look to those on the outside and how the other person may misconstrue your attention. Follow the rules that you know."

Kamden smiled at his grandfather. "What happened with the other girl?"

Papa checked his pole. "Well, your Mama Crystal asked me not to speak with her, or any other girl, on social media. However, one week later, the young lady sent me a text message about some products she was selling, which Mama Crystal happened to see. She sent the girl a text message a few minutes later and asked her to stop texting me. She said that she had seen some inappropriate conversations between us. She let her know that she had already asked me to stop talking to her, but she wanted to ask her, woman to woman, to never contact me again. I felt it was overkill, but it worked.

"Sadly, it doesn't stop there," Papa continued nervously. "I used to have a wondering eye. I am not even sure why I would do it, but if I saw a pretty girl, my eyes would just follow her. That is a mis-statement. I knew why I was doing it. I was letting my flesh control my mind's eye. It is truly a daily walk, son. We must pray daily over our minds. We have to die out to this stinking flesh every day. Once at a restaurant, your ever-diligent Mama Crystal called me out. She said she noticed my wondering eye and was curious if I ever thought about how it made her feel.

"Sometimes, in marriage, our spouses can see our deepest darkest sins. Of course, this goes both ways. But, they know where we struggle the most. It is all a part of becoming one. And, to help, they will expose them, in love. Which, of course, is exactly what I needed in this situation.

"When she first started riding in the truck with me, she called me out again. I had been watching a certain show on my phone during my downtime. I knew the show wasn't exactly good, but I didn't see anything too terribly wrong with it.

"I wasn't in the best place spiritually at the time. The show was full of violence and cursing. In the middle of an episode, she said that the show was messing with me spiritually. I became enraged. We had a major argument. I couldn't understand why I had gotten so angry until later when the Lord replayed her words to me and I realized that there was a spiritual war happening. He had given me a wife who was helping me fight for my soul.

"In my laziness, I had let my guard down and that angry spirit, I was picking up from that awful show and that I naturally had as a man, was causing me to be in a foul mood most days and argue with the one person I had promised to love and protect.

"Interestingly, I found that the closer I got to God, the less I cared about anything that was displeasing to Him. I loved your Mama Crystal. I loved her tenacity and the desire she had for both us to make it to Heaven.

"She prayed for me often. I sure do miss her." Papa wiped tears from his eyes. "She always said that I helped her spiritually, but I am not sure if I ever expressed how much she helped me."

Kamden reeled in a fish and gave his Papa a smile. "Yes, sir. We all do. I am so glad that you two were able to get past those issues. I am sure we could all benefit from more practical teaching in this area."

He grabbed the Bible. "Whoso findeth a wife findeth a good thing and obtaineth favour of the Lord" (Proverbs 18:22).

Papa smiled. "Amen and Amen. Call Joy, son. Make this right. We aren't promised tomorrow, and I can tell you from experience that any time spent out of your wife's good graces is wasted time."

Kamden packed up his pole. "I'll do better than that, Papa. I'm going to grab her some flowers and take her to dinner. I am going to listen to her side and then we are going to work together to find a way to make sure neither of us is ever put in another position like this.

"You know, Papa, men and woman hardly ever have real discussions about these issues. It may be something to look into. Maybe I could host a real man-to-man conference or something. We need to hear these things at every age from adolescence on up. The problem would be finding men bold and passionate enough to be real about issues and situations like this that they have faced. If I can get it together, do you think you could speak?" Kamden was clearly excited.

Papa let out a long sigh. "I suppose I could. I wonder if some of the issues I faced could have been avoided with more practical teaching."

Kamden started jotting down notes. "Yes, Joy and I have discussed the need for a candid series on marriage. As Christians, we need to be able to discuss real-life issues as they relate to this walk of holiness."

Papa chimed in, "Yes, I am quite certain there are many who may not have a good grasp of these subjects. Perhaps they couldn't speak openly with parents or, like me, didn't grow up in truth. As a young man, new to the faith, I remember having many questions about how to live in contrast to the world I once knew. Yes, son, if you arrange it, I will be there. I guess this old bag of bones still has something to give the kingdom." Papa rose to leave. "To God be the glory."

Kamden said a quick goodbye and began to plan this exciting new adventure.

As he made his way back to the house, Papa smiled and thanked God. "Look at you, Lord, sending him purpose and passion. You have taken his mind off his troubles and pointed it right back to Yourself. I know You are in control."

***

It was from this conversation that the Real Man, and later the Real Apostolic Marriage, Conferences were born. I know those here who have attended enjoy these meetings as much as I do.

We have seen many marriages healed. So many questions have been asked and answered in these conferences. They truly help us all to be better Christians. But, it took an honest conversation from a man who wasn't ashamed to admit that he had messed up and didn't know it all to initiate the spark.

The winds of change often begin to blow when we are able to get honest with ourselves, each other, and God.

Behind his warm smile, Papa Jones was a man who had learned to live in submission, and be honest about what got him there.

"And moreover, because the preacher was wise, he still taught the people knowledge; yea, he gave good heed, and sought out, and set in order many proverbs.

The preacher sought to find out acceptable words: and that which was written was upright, even words of truth. The words of the wise are as goads, and as nails fastened by the masters of assemblies, which are given by one Shepard. And further, by these, my son, be admonished: of making many books there is no end; and much study is a weariness of the flesh. Let us hear the conclusion of the whole matter: Fear God, and keep his commandments: for this is the whole duty of man. For God shall bring every work into judgement, with every secret thing, whether it be good, or whether it be evil" (Ecclesiastes 12:9-14) .

At this time, we will allow a few of our family and friends gathered today to come and share what Papa Jones meant to them. Please be mindful of the allotted timeframe. Following this, I will return to close us out with a few more remarks.

***

"Kamden, are you ok?" Papa made his way into the study with two cups of coffee.

Kamden looked up from his Bible. "Yes, Papa. I am just wondering how we are going to get past this tough spot. Things seemed to be going so good and now this. I am just not sure what can be done to prevent a major catastrophe at the church."

Papa Jones took a seat next to the desk. "Well, son, I am sure God has already made a way of escape. I know it looks hopeless, but that is not what it looks like to Him. We need to ask Him what He is trying to teach you in this season. I am sure there is a lesson in here somewhere."

Kamden shook his head and pulled out a binder. "Yes, I know all the clichés, but they aren't helping right now. I have been praying and fasting along with everyone else. I, too, believe the answer is coming. It is just hard to wait on its arrival when all you see is doom."

Papa stirred his coffee and reached for Kamden's Bible. "I know too well the fiery trial, son. I am not sure if I ever shared this with you, but there was a time that I thought there was no way out for me.

"When I first started Apostolic Trucking, we had three years of growth. The business seemed to be going in a wonderful direction. Your Mama Crystal had just left her job to ride with me full time, and I had gotten my second truck. I also had another driver leased to me. Somewhere during that three-year span, I lost track of the mission of my trucking company.

"I stopped seeing God in it and was just looking for dollar signs. I told myself, and everyone else, that God was my end game, but I wasn't conducting myself like that. I saw the money our drivers and lessees were making and I coveted it. I wanted to make those dollars for myself.

"This was about the time your Aunt Terry and Uncle Jake were headed off to college. I started taking out these easy money business loans. They gave us cash on hand to expand, but with ridiculous interest rates. They were a sham and I fell for it. Then God pulled the rug out from under me.

"I can see now why, but then it was painful. We almost lost everything. Mama Crystal and I would often just look at each other and shake our heads. We could see God all during the madness, but we had to pray for Him to help our unbelief. We were powerless to do anything to get our heads above water, but He never failed us."

"While we were busy conquering territory for the kingdom, we lost the leased driver, and my driver wrecked one of my trucks causing several thousands in damage. I went from a three-truck operation to a one-truck operation almost overnight. We also had two kids in Bible college at the time and a never-ending amount of bills piling up. I owed all these loan companies daily payments that I could no longer make. We didn't have two pennies to rub together and lived in fear of losing everything daily. I believe the power and water were cut off at one point.

"One Sunday, our Pastor came over and said the Lord had given him a word for us about our business. He said he felt impressed to tell us about a time when he was in Bible college and he was doing everything himself, trying to make sure it was all perfect, and his mentor asked him which man is better: A man that works like ten men or the one who puts ten men to work." Papa smiled. "Sometimes God sends someone with a simple word that gives you something to hold on to in the hard times."

"I told the Pastor a little about what we were going through and thanked him for the word. That small word from the Lord propelled me into a new direction. Instead of being scared and frustrated. I just accepted that this was the season we were in and got to work. I knew that my passion and goal for the company was Godsent.

"I wanted to put men to work in a godly business. There wasn't an instant answer. We didn't get a miracle check in the mail. There was no anonymous donation. But we did have a new determination to make it. We had to encourage each other often. I had to work hard. We had to pray and fast and truly believe what we were living for. Knowing God will make a way and trusting Him to do so are two different things. There were so many days I couldn't see past the negative bank account and get over the bill collector's constant calls.

"I would begin to plan my own way of escape or become frustrated and your Mama Crystal would look over at me and, very quietly, say 'just trust Him.' I would use that to press on. There were days I would look over and she would look so worried, and I would remind her to trust Him.

"It is truly a scary feeling for a man to not know how he will feed his family. I wanted to be a man of character and run my business with integrity. I hated not being able to pay my bills on time. For a time, Mama Crystal had to come out of the truck and get a job. But, God never let us down. The Lord was with us the whole time. There were many days our account would be negative and then He would supply a load just in time to make the tuition or truck insurance payments.

"Neither of us stopped working for the Lord. We were in the heat of a fiery trial, but continued to do what we knew to do, mainly because we didn't know what else to do. We also believed that only what is done for Jesus truly matters. We knew that God hadn't left us, but we couldn't understand why we were going through such a terrible time. It is one thing to hear great sermons on trusting God or try to inspire new converts to believe in His power, but to be in the trial and try to trust Him is something completely different. I know that because we hung on in those moments God continued to bless and prosper the business.

"He is the reason that we even have a company today. We had to shut down the business for a short time during this season. I felt like a complete failure. I couldn't pay the bills without my wife's help. I had to go back to work for someone else. I was humiliated and unsure of my next move. It was in this season that I truly learned what it is to lean on the Lord and not to my own understanding.

"What I am trying to tell you is not a cliché; it is a testimony of God's grace and mercy. His unchanging hand is always with His people. We don't always know how, we very rarely know the why, but we can trust in the who." Papa smiled at his grandson.

The Bible says, "Now no chastening for the present seemeth to be joyous, but grievous: nevertheless, afterward it yieldeth the peaceable fruit of righteousness unto them which are exercised thereby" (Hebrews 12:11).

***

I love that Papa Jones never sugar-coated things for me. His stories were real and raw. They made me look at myself and helped me to understand the man I so admired.

I had to see him in the light of his fears and failures and love him as he was, just a man saved by grace. His battles were different than mine because he came from the world. But, through them, I learned to appreciate the presence and grace of the Lord in my own life.

I could hear a story from him and it would make me question my stance on certain issues. I would have to go back to the Word, as he always did, and make sure I was living in the light of the Bible.

Through him, I learned to examine every relationship in my life. I want to make sure I appreciate, to the fullest, the blessings in my life and take the time to prune the unproductive areas.

For all of us who knew Papa Jones, his smile and laugh, and the simple way he served, let us hold on to these things as we feel his loss today.

6
TO EVERYTHING A SEASON

"Papa, do you feel like heading down to the pond? I could bring some poles for us to drop in the water." Kamden was hoping to get his aging grandfather out of the house for a little while. "Or maybe we could head over to the church. Joy has been updating my office. I am sure you will love the changes she has made. She has a special shelf on the wall by the door to display all of Mama Crystal's books."

Papa Jones smiled at his grandson. "Son, I know you have much more important things to do than cart this old bag of bones around. I am fine right here. I will just read for a while and catch a nap. I would like to see a picture of Mama Crystal's books on display. I know that they are blessing souls now just as they did when she wrote them."

Kamden shook his head in agreement. "Of course, they are. And, for your information, I would like nothing more than carting your old bag of bones around for the day. My schedule is clear until late this evening. The new Youth Pastor will be starting next week. He will be here on Saturday for dinner. I can't wait for you to meet him. I believe he will be so good for our students. You wouldn't believe all of the wonderful references I received about him."

Papa grabbed his Bible from the coffee table. "Oh, yes. I have heard good things as well. I have been praying for God to show you His will for the next generation. I can remember so vividly you and little Ariel running around here excited about Children's Church. Throw Kathy in the mix and you three were quite a sight.

"Now, you are all grown with families of your own. The circle of life sure doesn't take long to get around. I was just reading this morning, 'But Jesus said, Suffer little children, and forbid them not, to come unto me: for such is the kingdom of Heaven'" (Matthew 19:14).

Papa smiled. "I am so thankful God has given you a burden for the next generation. You know Mama Crystal and I came from the world into this glorious truth. We weren't raised knowing about repentance, baptism in the name of Jesus, and the infilling of the Holy Ghost. Papa turned to Acts Chapter 2. "Now when they heard this, they were pricked in their heart, and said unto Peter and to the rest of the apostles, Men, and brethren, what shall we do? Then Peter said unto them, repent, and be baptized every one of you in the name of Jesus Christ for the remission of sins, and ye shall receive the gift of the Holy Ghost" (Acts 2:37-38).

Papa was moved to tears. "It was always our desire to live in a way that would help the generations of our family coming after us know the Lord from an early age. I always guarded and coveted my walk with the Lord because I didn't want to do anything to hinder that dream.

"To sit here now and see the way you have all turned out makes my soul sing." Papa closed his Bible and looked up at Kamden "Son, you go ahead and spend time with that beautiful family you have in the other room. I think I will head down to the pond for a bit."

Kamden looked a little concerned. "Are you sure you can make it down there ok? I could walk down with you for a bit and come back for you later."

Papa shook his head. "No, no. I will be fine. I would quite enjoy the alone time. Now you go on and kiss those lovely kiddos for me."

***

That was the last time I ever spoke with him. He walked down to the lake with his pole in one hand and his tackle box in the other.

When we found him several hours later, his pole was in the water and the tackle box was open with his Bible laid out on top of it. God let him pass in his favorite place doing one of his favorite things.

He used to tell me that he heard a preacher say once that fishing was God's sport. He had made us all fishermen.

I don't know what I could or would have said to him had I known it was to be our last conversation. Can we ever know that? I read in Mama Crystal's first book, "A Life Altar'd," that she had the same questions when her beloved Granny had passed.

The circle of life doesn't take long to get around. That was on his mind on that last day.

Papa Jones started his life in the country in the deep south of Georgia. He always had a big smile on his face when he spoke of this season of life. He made a transition to the big city of Atlanta after the passing of his mother as a teenager.

He found the city hard and unforgiving. It was in this time that he lost himself and found the Lord. After serving his time in prison, he became a servant of the Lord. He worked hard to know the Lord and develop his calling. He preached red-hot revivals and served his local congregation until he lost himself again.

He spent several years running from the Lord. He was dodging the shame he felt for not making it. Then he found himself back in the open arms of a loving and forgiving Savior. This would be the last time he would walk away.

Of course, there were times he failed, sinned, or became cold, but he never walked away. He always had a repentant heart and love for the truth. He found the family God intended him to have. He loved his wife and children, was faithful to his church and ministry, and worked hard as the Lord provided the strength. He ran a successful business that still provides an Apostolic witness to truckers across America.

As wonderful a man as he was, he was just a man. If you are here today and feeling like you aren't on the right track, or in the right place with God, please know that there is hope. God doesn't expect you to be like Papa Jones, or me; He expects you to be like Him. That is our journey as Christians, to become more like Him every day.

The world and many religions today are focused on you knowing and accepting Christ. But, the real focus should be on whether or not He knows us. Are we living lives that are in alignment with His Word? Do our daily activities please our Lord and maker? The Word tells us that, "Thou believest that there is one God; thou doest well: the devils also believe, and tremble" (James 2:19).

If you know and believe in Him, that is great. It is a wonderful place to start. But, to make it to Heaven, He must know you. The Word tells us that when the judgment comes, many will stand before Him *and say all the wonderful things they have done in His name; but, He will tell them to depart because He never knew them.*

Pastor, how do we know if He knows us? That is a good question. He knows us if we are in a relationship with Him. First, we must be born again through repentance, baptism in Jesus name, and the infilling of the Holy Ghost with the evidence of speaking in tongues. Then we must live a life dedicated and separated unto Him. Living this life takes the disciplines of prayer, Bible reading, fasting, and living a sanctified life. We must live on purpose. No matter where you are in this journey, God is here today and can, and will, meet you where you are at.

Any day is a good day to meet or reconnect with the Lord. Papa would have wanted his goodbye service to this world to be someone else's hello moment with Jesus.

Before Aunt Terry comes to close us out in song, I would like to share one last passage of Scripture with you. Papa's Bible was open to this Psalm when he took his last breaths. It is no surprise to any of us who knew him, as it was one of his favorites.

In my best Papa Jones's voice, the Bible reads:

"O Lord, thou hast searched me, and known me. Thou knowest my downsitting and mine uprising, thou understandest my thoughts afar off.

Thou compassest my path and my lying down, and art acquainted with all my ways. For there is not a word in my tongue, but, lo, O Lord, thou knowest altogether.

Thou hast beset me behind and before and laid thine hand upon me. Such knowledge is too wonderful for me; It is high, I cannot attain unto it. Whither shall I go from thy spirit? Or whither shall I flee from their presence?

If I ascend up into heaven, thou art there: If I make my bed in hell, behold, thou art there. If I take the wings of the morning and dwell in the uttermost parts of the sea; even there shall thy hand lead me, and thy right hand shall hold me. If I say, surely the darkness shall cover me; even the night shall be light about me.

Yea, the darkness hideth not from thee; but the night shineth as the day: the darkness and the light are both alike to thee. For thou hast possessed my reins: thou hast covered me in my mother's womb. I will praise thee; for I am fearfully and wonderfully made: marvelous are thy works; and that my soul knoweth right well.

My substance was not hid from thee, when I was made in secret, and curiously wrought in the lowest parts of the earth. Thine eyes did see my substance, yet being unperfect: and in thy book all my members were written, which in continuance were fashioned, when as yet there was none of them.

How precious also are thy thoughts unto me, O God! How great is the sum of them!

If I should count them, they are more in number than the sand: when I awake, I am still with thee. Surely, thou will slay the wicked, O God: depart from me, therefore, ye bloody men.

For they speak against thee wickedly, and thine enemies take their name in vain. Do not I hate them, O Lord, that hate thee? And am not I grieved with those that rise up against thee? I hate them with perfect hatred: I count them mine enemies.

Search me, O God, and know my heart: try me, and know my thoughts: and see if there be any wicked way in me, and lead me in the way everlasting" (Psalms 139).

Epilogue

Though some of the stories in this book are fictional or exaggerated, the premise and the man are very real.

My husband grew up in rural South Georgia. He was loved by his parents and loved his country roots. His mother passed away when he was a teenager and he subsequently moved to the city of Atlanta.

It was during this time that he was introduced to the dark side of city life. He began doing, and eventually selling, drugs. He also had issues with women. His misadventures in this new world landed him in jail several times.

During one long stint in the county jail, as he was being prepared to go down the road (head off to prison), he got into some trouble inside the jail. But, God had a plan, as He always does. My husband made a deal with God. If He would keep him out of this impending punishment, he would start hanging out with the saved crowd and learn more about Him.

He was true to his word; he started reading the Bible and attending any service that the county jail offered. Later, while in prison, he read in the book of Acts about the Holy Ghost. One afternoon, on the prison yard, his buddies told him to lift his hands and ask God to fill him. He lifted his arms and began to shout "Hallelujah." Before he knew it, he was speaking in tongues.

Fast forward a few years, he got out of prison, got married, and found a church home. God had given him the spirit of an evangelist. He was licensed in his local Apostolic assembly and began his work for the ministry in his early twenties. He preached a revival once and his grandmother received the gift of the Holy Ghost; what an honor.

However, being a young man, he didn't treasure the position he had been placed in as much as he should have. When she was almost twelve years old, he found out that he had a daughter. He worked hard to form a bond with her from the start.

Slowly, one concession at a time, he began to backslide or fall away from the Lord. It was during this time that he started his trucking company, Apostolic Trucking; but, like everything else in his life, it eventually came crashing down. He found himself divorced, separated from his church and ministry, bankrupt, and lost without God.

God was still there, but he wasn't looking for Him. He spent a few years in this state. He tried to come back to God on his own terms, but that isn't how God wants it to be. He visited different churches. When his girlfriend became pregnant, he tried to do the right thing and marry her, but that didn't happen. None of his attempts to make his life right were working out.

After the birth of his second daughter, he realized he needed God. He was at a low point and couldn't find hope or the ability to rise above in himself. He had heard about an Apostolic Pentecostal Church that was near the trailer park where he lived.

After just a few visits, he found himself at the altar crying out to God and speaking in that beautiful Heavenly language of the Holy Ghost.

He was determined to never stray from the Lord again. He began attending the church and was thrilled to introduce his oldest daughter to his new friends when she visited.

During this time, he started praying for a godly wife. He secretly hoped that he could make things work with the baby's mom, but it seemed impossible. She wasn't interested in the fact that he had suddenly gotten deeply religious and made seeing his daughter very difficult for him at first.

Being a long-haul trucker made regular church attendance impossible, but he was faithful anytime he was at home. One day, one of the ladies at the church invited him to a youth prayer service that was at another member's home. He enjoyed the fellowship and met many new faces. One, in particular, would be very important in the near future, as he was his soon-to-be step-son.

During this meeting, another young lady invited him to the homeless ministry. He was informed to be at the church at six am that coming Saturday. He immediately fell in love with this ministry.

After preparing sack lunches, the team carpooled downtown to have service with over two hundred homeless people. They had been doing this for over ten years and never missed a Saturday. The young lady that had invited him asked if he wanted to ride to the city with her and her roommate. The roommate shared her powerful testimony, which inspired him to share his.

He was a little leery of how he would be perceived once these young ladies found out he was an ex-con. But, they never batted an eye. In fact, they invited him out to street evangelism following homeless ministry.

Now, these were his kind of people. He remembered the good old days when he used to work diligently for the Lord. He agreed to meet them later to Take the Streets, as they called their team. That roommate was me. And the rest, you could say, is history.

You can read more about us in my first book, *A Life Altar'd*.

I wanted to share a little of the real Papa Jones with you to confirm the life-changing power of Jesus Christ.

My husband is a man that deals with the flesh. I meant every high accolade I have given him; however, he has to take up his cross daily. We are not overcomers because we win a battle with sin. We are made overcomers in the daily walk with the Lord. We are admonished to take up our cross daily. Living for the Lord is a daily walk. God will do what we can't do, but He will never do what we can do. That is our job.

As born again, blood-bought Christians, we are commanded to live on purpose. He has a plan for us, even when following Him is the last thing on our minds.

Also, I hope to reinforce the truth that we are all made overcomers by the words of our testimony.

In closing, I would like to share this passage of Scripture with you from the word of God:

"Finally, my brethren, be strong in the Lord, and in the power of his might. Put on the whole armour of God, that ye may be able to stand against the wiles of the devil. For we wrestle not against flesh and blood, but against principalities, against powers, against the rulers of the darkness of this world, against spiritual wickedness in high places. Wherefore take unto you the whole armour of God, that ye may be able to withstand in the evil day, and having done all, to stand. Stand therefore, having your loins gird about with truth, and having on the breastplate of righteousness; and your feet shod with the preparation of the gospel of peace; above all, taking the shield of faith, wherewith ye shall be able to quench all the fiery darts of the wicked. And take the helmet of salvation, and the sword of the Spirit, which is the word of God; praying always with all prayer and supplication in the Spirit…"(Ephesians 6:10-18)

ABOUT THE AUTHOR

Crystal Jones is happily married. They have four children, a daughter-in-law, and two grandchildren. She has been a regular member of her local UPCI, Apostolic Pentecostal Church, for the past ten years.

The following is one of her favorite portions of Scripture:

"Seek ye the Lord while he may be found, call ye upon him while he is near: let the wicked forsake his way, and the unrighteous man his thoughts: and let him return unto the Lord, and he will have mercy upon him; and to our God, for he will abundantly pardon. For my thoughts are not your thoughts, neither are your ways my ways, saith the Lord" (Isaiah 55:6-9).

www.ingramcontent.com/pod-product-compliance
Lightning Source LLC
Chambersburg PA
CBHW020954030426
42339CB00005B/103